Hailstorm Interlude

poems by

Thomas J. Erickson

Finishing Line Press
Georgetown, Kentucky

Hailstorm Interlude

Copyright © 2018 by Thomas J. Erickson
ISBN 978-1-63534-724-1 First Edition
All rights reserved under International and Pan-American Copyright Conventions. No part of this book may be reproduced in any manner whatsoever without written permission from the publisher, except in the case of brief quotations embodied in critical articles and reviews.

ACKNOWLEDGMENTS

"Baseball" appeared in *The Pacific Review*.
"Blue" appeared in *Verse-Virtual*.
"Boats" appeared in *Hartskill Review*.
"Discovery" appeared in *Rat's Ass Review*.
"On the Incline of a Dune" appeared in *Panoply*.
"The Prison Visit" appeared in *Verse-Virtual*.
"The Providence of the Fall of a Snowflake" appeared in *Blue River Review*.
"The Theft" appeared in *Stoneboat*.
"Undertow" appeared in *Bramble*.
"Van Gogh's Ear" appeared in the *2018 Wisconsin Fellowship of Poets' Calendar* and *The Pacific Review*.
"Willow Glen" appeared in *Verse-Virtual*.

Publisher: Leah Maines
Editor: Christen Kincaid
Cover Art: Jeffrey Jensen
Author Photo: Thomas J. Erickson
Cover Design: Elizabeth Maines McCleavy

Printed in the USA on acid-free paper.
Order online: www.finishinglinepress.com
also available on amazon.com

Author inquiries and mail orders:
Finishing Line Press
P. O. Box 1626
Georgetown, Kentucky 40324
U. S. A.

Table of Contents

Hailstorm Interlude ... 1
At the Monkey Skull Museum ... 2
The Other Tom ... 3
The Theft ... 4
At the Abandoned Lumberjack Cemetery ... 6
Undertow ... 7
Blue ... 8
Discovery ... 10
The Prison Visit ... 12
Presumption of Innocence ... 13
The Eclipse ... 14
The Weave ... 15
Boats ... 16
Baseball ... 17
Considering Stormy Day by Milton Avery Because I Feel Obligated to Write a Poem to Enter in an Ekphrastic Poetry Competition ... 18
Van Gogh's Ear ... 19
If Tobe Hooper Is Dead Who the Fuck Is Still Alive ... 20
Night Moves ... 21
Willow Glen ... 23
Getting Busy ... 24
Love Song ... 25
The Providence of the Fall of a Snowflake ... 26
The Relative Happiness of a Biped in Comparison to Bobbleheads ... 27
On the Incline of a Dune ... 28
Elegy for All Those Thousands of Souls Who Wrote Poems that No One Will Ever Read but Who Loved Poetry Just as Much as Randall Jarrell or Marianne Moore or Your English Professor in College Ever Did ... 29
November ... 30

Hailstorm Interlude

"What the hell was that?" asked
    my dog in the middle
of the night. I said, "It's hail hitting
    against the window."
"What the hell is hail?" he demanded.
    "Don't worry about it. Let's
try to go back to sleep." He cuddled
    in next to me but
now I had to go to the bathroom. I sat
    there looking at the scores
on my cell phone when my mom, who
    had been dead for a couple
of years, called and told me to get out
    my baseball card collection.
I located my Clete Boyer from 1966. It
    was the last card I needed to
complete my checklist, and I found it
    in a pack I bought in a drug
store in Chippewa Falls, Wisconsin, for
    a nickel when I was six.
By the time I crawled back into
    bed the hailstorm had stopped.
"Where were you? I was getting a little
    worried," said the pooch.
I told him about the phone call
    and the baseball card and how
finding it was one of the happiest moments
    of my life but when I waited for
his reaction, all I could hear was his light
    snoring. The sun started to come
up, and the birds started to sing, and I
    pretended they had heard what
I was talking about.

At the Monkey Skull Museum

The skull of the pygmy marmoset is the size
of one of those plastic mini football helmets
my dad would get for me for free with a fill-up
of a tank of gas at Citgo. The bone is so
thin it would be like breaking the crust of crème
brule to get to the tasty brain whether by talon
or claw or spoon.

You can see the faint line of plate fusion
dividing the skull of the tufted capuchin.
A marking as delicate and fine as a painted
horizon line on the glaze of a Grecian amphora.

The one that looks the most human is the bonobo.
Its skull looks eerily similar to Norman Bates'
mother when her bewigged visage turns toward
Vera Miles below the dangling light bulb.

Hitch said blondes make the best victims because
they're like bloody footprints in virgin snow. He
liked his icy blondes but he was irritated when
Vera got pregnant so he gave the good part
to Janet Leigh who's now forever immortalized
for being stabbed in the shower. Hitch knew
the value of women.

My wife keeps talking about how she wants to go now.
She's had enough of this museum.

There's this "universal phenomenon" of men inter-
rupting women which I suppose started four million
years ago when humans split from monkeys. I'm not
going to interrupt her because I am, all of a sudden, sympathetic.

The Other Tom

> *Most people are other people.*
> Oscar Wilde

I've been stepping out of myself lately.
I'm not sure why but I think I may espy,
if I bide my time, Tom doing something.
I have a quiet sense that a deep revelation
is at hand.

It's a Saturday afternoon in late September.
I watch Tom dump the hanging baskets
in the compost bin and jimmy the shepherd's
poles out of the dry ground. He pauses
and looks around and decides to put
the garden hose in the garage. He comes back
to the garden and picks up the stone frog—
the one holding the green orb--and hurls it
across the backyard and beyond.

Then, Tom walks back to the house where,
I assume, he asks his wife if she's ready
to take the dog for a walk.

The Theft

When my ex-wife sold her house,
the one I gave her in the divorce,
I went to the backyard and dug up
some peonies and bluebells (which
sort of felt like they were still mine)
to transplant in my own garden.
It was kind of heavy work what
with the swing set still there
and the bird bath filled with twigs.

On my way home, I was pulled
over by the police who suspected
I was up to no good. They asked
me where I got those flowers and
I said at my house on Sheffield.
They said you don't live on
Sheffield anymore. I said I know
but I used to and that should count
for something. They drove me back
over and said I'd better prove I
used to live there or I was going
to jail. I told them to go upstairs
and look for a latch behind where
the big oak desk used to be. Open
the latch and you'll find a storage
area and inside there will be a cardboard
box with all my old LPs.
They brought the box down and
asked how do we know these are
your records, it could have been
a lucky guess. I told them take out
the Elvis Costello album
and you'll find a fragment of an unfinished
poem I wrote on the white

sleeve in my almost indecipherable
scrawl. I'm going to have to read it
to you:

In the livid twilight, you hold
my arm while crossing the icy street.
We crush berries in the snow—
red on white.

Warm for awhile.
Coffee and eggs are a comfort.
You, across the table,
turn away
to watch the snow fall

and the snow falls
so silently

They let me go.

This spring the bluebells didn't come up
but the peonies will be in bloom by May.

At the Abandoned Lumberjack Cemetery

Outside the town of Seney in the Upper Peninsula
of Michigan, I am with my two young sons
at a forgotten cemetery on one of those
August afternoons before school starts
when you try to wring out one more
cool thing to do before the end of summer.
It is late in the afternoon but the sun is still
high so far north and the shadows
of the tree branches fall over
the clearing like gathering tendrils.

The ground of several graves
has fallen into depressions
a few feet deep as the wooden boxes
and bones have returned to the sandy
muck. As a joke, I lie down in one
of the holes in the ground. For a while,
I hear the boys scampering about
and then it turns quiet and I know
they have followed my lead
lying still in their own
sunken beds of cool grass.

While we lie there looking at the sky
wars are being fought,
ice caps are melting,
languages are becoming extinct,
my sons are growing older

where time is now beyond time
where if only we could stay.

Undertow

There's a boy I know

or maybe not

who asked why

join a team

or go to a dance

and I said

that's what kids do…

Did you?

I said let's drive

to the pier to

swim in the waves

The wind was from

the northwest

Blue

I leave my white town,
to drive to the black crime
scene in the black neighborhood
where my black client maybe
shot the black girl on the porch
of the house where the blood
stain has turned black.

I take notes in my white
notebook amid the white
noise of the radios and insects
and passing cars and then on
to my office in the white
Third Ward with the white
bars and white restaurants
where I talk to my white
friends about the black men
who played basketball
in front of the white
crowd last night on tv.

Later, I go to the jail and
pass by the white jailers
to talk to my black client
about the charge of the black
on black crime brought by
the white DA before we go
in front of the white judge
and eventually the white
jurors who live in their white
enclaves leading their white
lives and afterwards I'll
talk to his black family

about the time he will serve
in the black prison up north
with the white prison guards

and then I'll drive home
past the white park to my house
in the white part of town
and relax and listen to the black
saxophonist who will turn
me blue for awhile before
I go to bed to dream my
colorless dreams.

Discovery
> *In criminal law: Process by which the prosecution gives information to the defendant's attorney regarding evidence supporting the charges against his client.*

Case #1

Cuz brought the two little boys up from Mississippi.
Mom was supposed to come once they got settled
but she stopped answering their calls.

After Cuz's boyfriend was arrested, they moved in with Solei.

Cuz tied up the boys so they wouldn't run away. Solei burned
them with cigarettes and beat them with a belt. No one fed them.
Cuz heard voices and loved to sing them to sleep.

The younger boy stopped breathing so Cuz took them to the hospital.

The one who lived told the police he loved Cuz.

Case #2

Sometime after midnight, they dragged the rapper to the basement
and choked him to death with a chain because he stole some weed.
They burned the body in a dumpster. A garbage truck dumped
the body in a landfill off Highway 45.

The rapper's blood was found in in the basement.
His DNA came back as female.

No one knew but his parents.

Case #3

His wife and kids barricaded the backdoor with a plastic picnic table, a garbage can, and a grocery cart found off the street but he busted through and poured gasoline around the kitchen and living room and lit a match.

He stopped at a gas station to call 911 but there was no pay phone. A guy who loaned him his cell phone recognized him from when they were in jail.

Two of the kids didn't make it out of the upstairs bedroom.
The boy was found draped over his little sister.

The Prison Visit

Because I'm an attorney and know where I'm going, I don't
need an escort to walk to the infirmary to see my guy
once I pass through security at the gatehouse.

A couple of inmates come up the path dressed in dark green. Neither
is one of my old clients but you never know. We don't make eye contact
but our shadows touch as we pass.

I am visiting Paul. He is paralyzed from the waist down and partially
blind after being shot by the cops. He has a little goatee which another
inmate has to shave. He's been in for twenty years and will die before
he makes parole. I don't want to lie so I don't bring it up.

He spends his days listening to music and lying in bed. He tells me
he's lucky because his room in the infirmary has a window. He can't
see much of anything but the light is different and sometimes
in the morning, the sun touches his face. He's begun listening
to classical music and really likes Vivaldi.

On the walk back to the gatehouse, I realize I probably won't see Paul
again. It's kind of a relief because I can't do anything for him anyway.
Plus, no one's paying me anymore. He'll die in his room someday.
His earphones will be in and no one will hear the symphony.

Presumption of Innocence

Sometimes it's the big things
that get my clients in trouble:
the fingerprint on the gun,
the surveillance video of the hand-to-hand,
the semen on the bedspread.

Sometimes it's the small things:
a strand of hair on a sweater,
an undeleted Facebook post,
a teardrop tattoo.

I like when the judge tells the jury
If you can reconcile the evidence upon any
reasonable hypothesis other than guilt
then you should find the Defendant not guilty
because it always makes me feel
like we, you and I (not me and some
anxious client), have a chance.

Sure, my fingerprints are everywhere,
not hearing you is part of my DNA,
and that tear in your eye falls too often.

But in the morning, I'll wake up
and take the dog for a walk, get
ready for work, bring you your coffee,
and kiss you good-bye. You'll smile
at me and we'll start the day.

The Eclipse

Between the blinking lighthouse
rising above the birches, pines,
and sand dunes five miles
to the east, and the pier with its
bright stanchion to the west,
an August beach fire is almost
a bonfire on Lake Superior.

The sun is setting in crimson
and Cherokee red and its reflection
beams toward us, parting the deep
blue water, beckoning us to walk on
its golden path into the blinding light.

Instead, we lie on our backs
as the stars come out one by one
like pin pricks through a sable
blanket, the contrails of the jets
like gleaming, evanescent rivers.

Last night we watched the lunar
eclipse, the moon to the south,
the pitched shadow falling on its
yellow canvas above Lonesome Point
from our vantage at the marina

where the fish station still stands and
where years ago my father cleaned
the trout caught from the pier while
I shivered in the moonlight, the lowing
of the foghorn echoing across the water.

The Weave

I follow my pass across court to the player on my right
who follows his pass to the player on his left who passes
to me and down the court we run. The basketball never
touches the floor and all that can be heard is the squeak

of tennis shoes and the thump of the ball from hand to hand
and its soft echo off the glass as it falls into the net and
to the hands of the next boy and on we go, three by three
by three, in this beautiful flowing river of teamwork and youth.

I'm wearing my Blue Bomber uniform and warming up
while the pep band is playing "Smoke on the Water"
and the home crowd and the band and I and the four other
boys from our town are merging into a collective consciousness
that is about to blow away the five boys from the other town.

After the game, I walk home in the cold Wisconsin night.
My mom is in the kitchen listening to the radio and kind
of half waiting for me to get home so she can ask me how
I played and if I'm hungry and do I want something to eat.

The ball's momentum always carries you forward to the next
pass, the next cut, the next goal. It's only when the ball drops
that you realize time is neither absolute nor fixed
but a mystical movement of memories running in and out,
back and forth, and on and on and on.

Boats

> *To be a poet is not my ambition, it's my way of being alone.*
> Fernando Pesson

From the pier
the straight-edge
of the horizon
balances an ore boat
in two dimensions

My brother wrote
"Joe and Cindy 1991"
in the drying concrete
years before my sons
and I jumped
into the cold water
of late summer

Now the lone line,
copper hook,
heavy sinkers

the low cool wind
from Canada

Cassiopeia ever
so faint
in the northern sky

Soon she will be
boasting of her beauty
while the empty boat
slowly falls away.

Baseball

Middle age is the enemy of art.
Orson Welles

The enemy of my writing, in my middle age, is baseball. I can watch baseball on TV all day long as if willing myself to some dangerous edge of absorption.

Why are some lefthander pitchers harder on righthanders than lefthanders? It's mind-boggling. Like a koan from Kung Fu. Tell me what is Buddha and then tell me why this pitcher's reverse splits defy all logic.

How come fastballs are averaging 91 mph when ten years ago they averaged 89 mph? The easy answer is PEDs but that doesn't make sense because everybody knows more players were taking steroids ten years ago then they are now. Baseball is clean, right little naïve Weedhopper? All I know is speed is up, runs are down, and A-Rod is still playing.

Why is the foul pole fair?

When I do go to games I always keep score. I didn't know why until I read the small type on the program: "Your scorecard will serve as a written memento and historical record of the game." So there.

It's better to stay home, to run home, to go home than go to the park because on TV you can watch the catcher give the signs to the pitcher. Give me a beer, let me sit in my blue chair with the windows open and, as night falls, anticipate the next pitch. The whole game could pivot on the next ten seconds 250 times a game. Man oh man oh man...

My grandfather lived by himself in a trailer at the end of a road in a little town where he played centerfield in his youth. At the end of his life, he was almost blind so he would sit right in front of the TV, lean in on his cane, and peer at the Tigers game. The closer he got to the screen, the easier it was to get lost in the rhythms of the game; the easier it was, in his old age, to let the imponderable be.

Considering "Stormy Day" by Milton Avery Because I Feel Obligated to Write a Poem to Enter in an Ekphrastic Poetry Competition

In the middle of the sea
a light breeze lifts the water
until it becomes
a wave. Its target, the lone gray
pier under the slate sky.

The wave's weak sisters threaten
to touch the shore with a rhythmic fall.
The beach is denuded and dark,
flattened into a piece of night.

The backdrop in the upper gallery
of the museum is Lake Michigan
where the ice floes gently undulate
above the rollers. Their gray not
so gray; their aim not so true.

Van Gogh's Ear

Here I sit on the grimy floor
in this hovel of a room in Arles.

I'm like a crimson conch listening
to the blaggards through the floor below me.

Pick me up, Vincent. Turn me proper,
put me to your other ear,
and listen to the calm of the ocean.

If Tobe Hooper Is Dead Who the Fuck Is Still Alive?

At the Star Dusk Drive-In on the south side
of Sheboygan, we sit on our lawn chairs
in front of the car with our cooler of chilly
boys and then, with the August gloaming
off Lake Michigan creeping in, "Texas Chainsaw
Massacre" begins and our two bucks are
suddenly worth it.

The dew on the windshield,
        The clacking of the chainsaw,
The beers bobbing in the melting ice,
        The steam of the bone off the blade,
The acrid smell of the ditch weed,
        The sun coming up on the cemetery,
The baseball practice looming tomorrow morning,
        The chainsaw held to the heavens.

Leather Face in my baseball glove.

Night Moves

When I saw Gene Hackman in the restaurant
in Santa Fe, I asked the waiter to pass him a note.
(I didn't want to intrude.) I hoped he could make
out my hen-scratching:
Please explain the ending to Night Moves. Tom

I could see that familiar grin he used to such
effect in "The Conversation" when his character
Harry was explaining how he bugged the hotel
room. The waiter said I could come over.

Gene said at the end of "Night Moves", he was
just a private eye trying to figure things out
and couldn't and I said, jeez Gene, that girl,
Jennifer Warren, was so great. Whatever happened
to her? He grinned again and told me when they were
filming in the Everglades she never wore underwear
and she drank a "shit load" of Diet Dr. Pepper.
"Fame, Tom, is a curious thing. The seventies
were before this new age where there is a fluidity
of personhood and where fame can be created, or
manufactured I suppose, through diffusion."

"Despite your elevated diction, Gene, I see
your point. Jennifer just didn't get the roles."

"Yeah, she had no other place to go. She drifted away."

At dusk, I drove out to Bandelier. The mule deer barely
stirred as I climbed the ladder to one of the abandoned
pueblos. I took out my jack knife and carved "Jennifer Warren"
into the ancient adobe wall just so someone would maybe
remember her.

Tonight, I have that same anxious feeling and it helps
me to think about the touchstones of my adolescence—
playing basketball outside at night where the metal nets
held the ball for a split second longer than the nets
in the gym and the light from the stanchions lit half
the court so I was playing in the light and in the dark
and in the in-between; fishing for brook trout with
my dad and brother in the narrow cold streams of
the Upper Peninsula and sometimes letting the rapids
take the line way downstream beyond where I couldn't
discern the snags or the holes but where there was
a thrill of having the bait travel low into the deep
unknown; and then I floated on to thoughts of my kids…

I dwell, at night, in a sweet fluidity on these things.
These things of my little rounded personhood.

Let it drift.

Willow Glen

I heard the empty pop can atop
his slightly opened door hit the floor,
the tread of his bare feet running
down the hall, then the alarm bell
of the front door. Darren was off
to the races and so was I.

He was sprinting to the 7-Eleven
again, a charged vision of chugging
soda sparking in his head. I tackled him
and we fell hard on the frozen ground.
He was heavy—no longer a little boy.
I gripped his arm and we trudged back
to the treatment center in the cold moonlight.

Once inside, I noticed that the knee
of Darren's sail-boated pajamas
was ripped and soaked with blood.
Hours later, in the emergency room,
we held him down while the doctor
stitched him up; Darren calmly following
the needle, in and out, in and out.
He uttered *Mountain Dew, Mountain Dew,*
over and over, like a Hindu mantra.
The peace which passeth all understanding.

At Christmas, when his parents visited
from New Jersey, Darren pulled out his stitches
his mouth gaping in a rictus of joy.

Getting Busy

Today at Home Depot, the old woman cashier
took a look at my four bags of red mulch and asked
if I was getting busy today. I said, well that depends
on what you mean by getting busy. Embarrassed,
she said, I meant in the garden and I said well that
would also depend on my wife. Then, she beeped my
four bags with her scanner. Each beep more gratifying
than the one before because I was closer to home
with every electronic sensation, each shot into the cloud.
I inserted instead of swiped , and as I was leaving
she surprised me and said oh you are going to get busy
today! I turned and said yes indeed I am getting busy,
God willing.

Love Song

Nothing is something
The product at the end of an equation
A Scrabble word
An alternative to everything
To everything that is everything

Nothing matters when we are
Swimming in Lake Superior
In August

Nothing matters

I believe in nothing

There is nothing I wouldn't do.

The Providence of the Fall of a Snowflake

On the Saturday night before Christmas,
I take the dog out for her last walk before bed.
The snow shimmers through the ambience
of the street lights like a slow-motion silver rain.

Hillocks of snow cap the posts
of the picket fences. The frosted birdhouses
sway in the wind.

The dog leads me through the neighborhood,
past quiet houses, the lights of the Christmas trees
warming the dark living rooms.

Close to home, her back paw freezes up
and she starts to limp. I take my gloves
off, hold her paw in my hands for a while,
and tell her she's a good girl and on we go.

It takes me a moment to realize the power
has gone out when I get home.

You've lit a few candles and put another
blanket on the bed. I make my way to you
in the silence and the shadows.

The Relative Happiness of a Biped in Comparison to Bobble Heads

On my shelf, there's an LA Ram probably bought at Lambeau Field in the 60s. His big plaster helmet head looks permanently to the right or to the west so he was looking back home even when his team got to St. Louis in 1996. Now, with his team returned to California, I imagine him looking beyond Los Angeles, out to the surfers and the breakers and the deep blue sea.

Lew Alcindor, stuck in time, before turning Muslim. No sky hook or Magic or Charlie Parker or Koran or convention speeches or coaching basketball on the Rez or writing books about the Rens. Oh, Bobble Head Lew, you are still in Milwaukee wearing your Bucks uniform, living at Juneau Village and dreaming of the coasts.

There's a bobble head of Carlos Gomez and one of Jean Segura, both Milwaukee Brewers. I got them in the summer of 2014 and, aside from their respective numbers of 9 and 27, they are the exact same bobble heads with the exact same face. 30 percent of the players in baseball are Latino. There is one Latino manager. If I turn Carlos and Jean, the two Dominicans, to face each other, would they laugh or cry?

Un-immortalized me and my un-immortalized dog take a walk tonight at dusk. The fireflies like rising stars from lawns and flower beds. The hum of dragonflies, an evensong in this vesper hour.

On the Incline of a Dune

A praying mantis
rests on a stalk
of long grass
the king
of his hidden world
arrayed in his
many-shaded greens
while the pine
grosbeaks rush
from copse to copse
finding seeds
in late September
before the winds
turn north.

Elegy for All Those Thousands of Souls Who Wrote Poems that No One Will Ever Read but Who Loved Poetry Just as Much as Randall Jarrell or Marianne Moore or Your English Professor in College Ever Did

Just know
death is nothing
more than another knot
on this string.
Just a thing
that happens next.

The caveman-beating-on-a-drum
sounds becoming language
the melting of words
into a poem.

November

My sons told me that November was coming
but I didn't believe them. There's no way
it will ever be November, I said. We're not
that stupid. Not here, this is America.

Now, when I meet up with my friends we don't
talk much about November even though it's
November and that's all we used to talk about.
We talk about sports and our kids and our work.
Before November, we prided ourselves on not
talking about our work, but there it is.

My wife doesn't like to watch the news during
November because November reminds her
of her father and her bosses who did things
to her in November during the years when
every month for her was November.

I sit at my desk and force myself to read
the stories about November in the paper.
Sometimes, I want to shout about November
but the guys I work with go through their lives
as if November never happened. I think they
think I'm crazy to worry so much about November.
Sometimes, I wonder if they even know it's
November.

November, though, is no time to be quiet--
not with wind whistling through the trees
and the leaves and dead branches waiting
to fall.

Thomas J. Erickson grew up in Kohler, Wisconsin. He received a Bachelor of Arts in English Composition from Beloit College and a law degree from Marquette University. He is an attorney in Milwaukee, where he is a member of the Hartford Avenue Poets. His award-winning chapbook, *The Lawyer Who Died in the Courthouse Bathroom* was published by Parallel Press of the University of Wisconsin Libraries in 2013. His full length poetry book, *The Biology of Consciousness*, was published in 2016 by Pebblebrook Press. He was nominated for a Pushcart Prize in 2016. He lives in Milwaukee with his wife, Daphne, and is the proud father of Charles and John.

www.ingramcontent.com/pod-product-compliance
Lightning Source LLC
LaVergne TN
LVHW041506070426
835507LV00012B/1376